Beginner's Guide to
PHOTOGRAPHY

Compiled by Jim Symonds

Henderson
Woodbridge, England *Publishing*

The word 'camera' is Italian and it means 'room'. Every modern day camera does indeed have a room — a light-tight box which contains the film!

Camera obscura

This was a tool used by artists dating back to the middle ages and beyond. It was a light-tight box with a convex lens at one end and a small hole at the other end. The artist would place an object in the box (say a vase of flowers) and a screen behind it that would reflect the image of the object. Then he would trace round it and colour it in!

Pioneer photographers

Some of the earliest photographers were WH Jackson, a Victorian explorer who never travelled anywhere without his camera, even the North pole, Roger Fenton, who fought in the Crimean War (1853-1856) and Mathew Brady who fought in the American Civil War (1861-1865).

Photography — Is it art?

A popular band of Victorian painters called the Pre-Raphaelites often took photographs of their subjects before painting them in order to make the picture eventually more realistic! Meanwhile, Victorian photographer Julia Margaret Cameron took photographs with specially softened lenses so that her pictures would look more like paintings!

The first snap!

The first snap was taken by the two men who made the first camera, in 1839. They were Louis Jacques Daguerre (a painter) and Joseph Nicéphore (a scientist). The picture was printed onto a special silver plate, called a Daguerro-type!

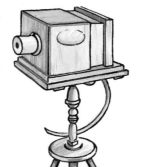

WHICH CAMERA?

Which camera?

All cameras work on the same principle but they can operate in different ways. There are four basic types of camera.

110, 126, viewfinder cameras

These cameras take good quality photographs and each has three different focus settings: head and shoulders — about one metre away; full body — about three metres away and landscape — anything over three metres. The lens that you look through is not the one that takes the photograph. There is normally a built-in flash.

35mm compact cameras

Here the quality of picture will be better even though the camera is fully automatic. The camera will focus for you, may even wind on the film automatically and rewind it at the end.

35mm single reflex cameras

This camera will produce the pictures of the best quality but they are easily the most expensive and can be quite tricky to use. Instead of looking through a viewfinder, you look through the lens, which you can change to suit your needs.

The disposable camera

Here the focus is pre-set when you buy the camera and there is already a film sealed inside. The camera is very cheap and, when you have taken your pictures, you send it to the processors and the photographs are returned to you...but the camera is thrown away!

WHICH FILM?

Here are answers to some common questions about film that will help you make the right choice when you buy film for your camera.

What types of film are there?

110, 126 or 35mm film. Each type is suitable for a particular camera (see previous page). You must get the film that is right for your camera.

How many exposures?

Normally the choice is 12, 24 or 36. This tells you how many pictures your film will take. You can normally manage to get one extra picture per film!

What is film speed?

This is what ASA means on the side of your film cassette. There are usually three film speeds: 100ASA, 200ASA or 400ASA. For general photography it is safer to buy 200ASA film.

Always take care when loading and unloading your film and always check that the film is winding on between shots.

There are three different types of film. It is a really good idea to try all three types at some time.

1. Colour print

This is the most common film and the one you are most likely to use. It can be processed easily and cheaply.

2. Slide film

This is generally more expensive to process than colour film. Sometimes the price includes the processing and your film comes with an envelope to send the film away in.

3. Black and white

Black and white is fun to use (see pages 31/32) but because so few people use it, the cost of processing is very high. It would pay to have a friend with their own darkroom because then you could process it yourself!

Holding a camera

1. Stand with your feet slightly apart and your elbows tucked into your body. This will help you take photographs that are not blurred!
2. Make sure that the camera strap is around your neck. Correct the length of the strap so that it is just right for your own size. Now it doesn't matter if you drop it!
3. When holding a camera, your weight should be evenly distributed. A balanced body means a steady hand!

Exposure

This is very important when taking a photograph. Exposure is the combination of aperture and shutter speed; the aperture is the size of the opening in the camera that the light goes through and the shutter speed is the length of time it is open. So if your photograph is under-exposed it is too dark and if it is over-exposed, it is too bright. Most cameras set the exposure automatically, so make sure your camera has fresh batteries!

This photograph has been under-exposed.

This photograph has been over-exposed.

In focus

If you have a compact camera, then it will focus the picture for you automatically. If, however, you have a single reflex camera, the focus is manual, ie. you have to do it yourself. Try to find something in your picture that you can focus easily on like a twig, a word on a sign or even a single human hair!

In focus photograph.

Out-of-focus photograph.

Composition

This means the way you arrange the 'subject' of your photograph. You must always make sure you like what you see before you press the button or else you waste a picture!

Choose your viewpoint

Do you want a bird's-eye view of a worm, or a worm's-eye view of a bird?

Choose your format

Does the subject of your picture require you to hold your camera vertically (eg. a face) or horizontally (eg. a river)?

Balance your picture

Divide the picture you see up into thirds. Does the most interesting part of the picture fall into the middle third?

Background

Make sure there is nothing in the background to spoil your composition; eg. a telegraph pole sticking out of the back of someone's head!

Foreground

Make sure there is nothing too bright in the foreground that will distract the subject of your composition, eg. a bright balloon in front of a pale, old man!

LANDSCAPES

Landscape photography relies heavily on the time of year and the time of day. The same view of a mountain can look completely different in May and October, as much as it can at dawn or dusk. As a photographer, you need to choose the correct conditions that will suit your picture. Take plenty of time looking for the right spot. The higher you go, the clearer the air, so the perspective improves.

Break the photograph down

Have something occurring in the foreground, the middle and the background. This gives the photograph depth and makes it a better picture.

Tripods

If the shutter speed is slower than 1/60th. of a second, you should use a tripod. If it is windy, put small stones around the legs of your tripod to give it more strength.

Cable release

If you are on a windy hill-top, then a cable release enables you to fire the shutter without actually touching the shutter, by use of a special cable. (See accessories, pages 47/48).

Filters

A filter is a tinted glass or plastic disc which fits onto the lens of a 35mm, or single reflex camera. Filters are very effective for landscape photography; they alter the way light affects film. You can buy different coloured filters for your camera. They enhance the beauty of skies, mountains, sunsets and other subjects of landscape photography.

Here are some examples of landscape
photography:

*Stubble burning on a late September
afternoon, a boy raking in the foreground and
smoke rising in the background give lots of
interest to this picture.*

*The sea
'landscape' is
disturbed by the
rope in the
foreground.
Without the rope,
the picture would
have been very
boring.*

*The soft evening
light brings out
the colours of
these cliffs. The
hut in the
foreground gives
depth to the
photograph.*

Cities are very exciting places to take photographs. It helps to know one well, but if not make sure you have a good, clear town or city plan. Don't snap up places of obvious beauty or famous landmarks. Instead, try to find really unusual places which other photographers might have passed by.

If you have a 35mm camera, then it helps to have a good zoom lens so you can get good close ups and candid shots. Always try to take photographs of buildings at unusual angles, or you may as well simply buy a postcard of it. Here are some city photographs:

Crowd scenes are nearly always exciting but here the crowd is silhouetted against the setting city sun to make the picture more dramatic. The sign is a focus of the picture and the lines of the back-to-back houses act as natural 'vanishing point' lines to make the picture look more 3-dimensional.

Try to catch people (and pets) unaware, going about their ordinary, everyday lives. Get as close as possible so that you fill up the frame with an interesting subject. If this picture had been taken horizontally, it would have been much less interesting because the subject would have been further away. ▶

Try and get in as close as you can. Remember you can use your camera vertically as well as horizontally. Choose contrasting subjects in your pictures; here we have a sweet shop next to a palm reader. Cities are filled with such contrasts, so make sure you find them! ◀

Slightly run-down areas of town are an interesting 'medium' for photography. ▶

Townscape Hints

* Use both colour and black and white film.
* Take pictures of similar scenes in different sorts of light.
* Try not to carry too many bags with you or you won't be free to move about the city as you wish.
* Wander down unknown streets. You never know what you might find to photograph.

All portrait photographs are either 'posed' or 'candid'. Posed means that the subject of your picture knows he or she is being photographed. Candid means that he or she doesn't know they are being photographed. Either method can produce great results — so that 'candid' pictures look as if they are 'posed', and 'posed' photographs can look as if they are 'candid'.

Posed portraits

Make sure that your subject is comfortable and relaxed. Try to photograph people in places they know, like a garden. Things to look out for:

Light: Do you want side-lighting, front-lighting or back-lighting?

Smile: Try to get your subject to smile. If this is difficult, ask him or her to blow their cheeks and to let out the air just before you press the shutter; this should cause a smile.

Activity: It helps if the subject of your picture is doing something, like reading a book or staring out to sea.

Take a vertical shot if it fits in with the shape of your subject. Try and make your portraits amusing. Here the ladder is an important part of the shape of the photograph. ▼

Look for an interesting background to bring out the best in your portrait. Have your subject at one side of the frame, instead of in the middle. ▶

Candid Portraits

You need to remember to have your camera with you at all times. The skill is to catch people unaware. You need to be patient and quiet. Try to carry spare film in case you run out at a crucial moment.

Side lighting can have a nice effect. Get as close as you can to your subjects. The background here enhances the faces of the happy couple.

An easy way to take a good candid picture is to come across people sleeping. Stand as close as you can. Your friend will get an awful shock when you show him the picture later! ▶

Special effects

* Put a light-coloured stocking over the lens. It will soften the look of the portrait.

* Photograph a face through frosted glass. A very ghostly effect!

MAKE A PINHOLE CAMERA

You can make your own camera at home that will give you lots of fun and also help you understand how 'real' cameras actually work. A pinhole camera is easy to make and you probably already have all the necessary equipment at home. So here goes!

What you need	Card
Glue	A pin
Scissors	Ruler
Tracing paper	Coloured pencils

What you do

1. Draw a net of a cube on a piece of card, making sure each face is 12cm by 12cm, as shown in the illustration. Also make sure you have drawn your tabs carefully as they are going to make your pinhole camera really strong.

2. Make two large pinholes in your net, as shown. Then, with some scissors cut a large cross in one of the faces, almost up to the edge. Carefully snip off the four triangles so that you have one hollow face, as shown.

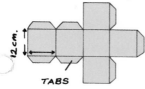

TABS

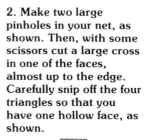

3. Glue along the edges of your hollow face and then stick a square of tracing paper over it. Press gently down at the sides until it is dry.

4. Make your cube. Squeeze each flap until it is dry. The last face will be a bit tricky, but patience is a virtue!

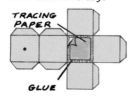

TRACING PAPER

GLUE

The image

You now have your own pinhole camera. Hold the pinhole towards an interesting view, such as a lovely, bright, sunny garden. Make sure your finger isn't covering the hole. Hold the camera well away from your eyes. It might even be best to have your arms at full length. Now if you look towards the 'viewfinder' (the face with the tracing paper) you will see an upside-down image of the garden that actually looks like a little colour photograph.

Always choose a view from which there is quite a lot of light coming — this is called 'a good light source'. This will always make your image brighter and better to see.

Why is the image upside down?

Because the light coming from the top of the view goes through the pinhole and touches the bottom of the tracing paper, and the light coming from the bottom goes to the top, as shown in this little diagram.

Is it possible to use real film with my pinhole camera?

Yes, but you would need to make a much more complicated camera and the picture that you would eventually get would be very disappointing. So the best thing to do is play happily with this one and take real photos with your real camera!

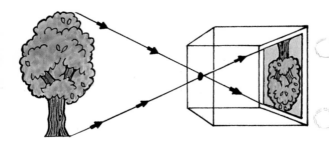

IN THE DARKROOM

These pages show you a simple way to make exciting pictures in your own darkroom without the help of an adult!

How to make your own darkroom
The best room to use is the one with the least number of windows. You can cover a window with dark, thick card and masking tape. For the door, find a big, old blanket and attach it to the door frame with drawing-pins. Turn off the light, and make sure you cannot see your hands!

What you will need
A darkroom safety light, which is usually red or orange; an angle-poise lamp with a bright bulb; black and white photographic paper; three photographic trays, each one a different colour — one for developer, one for fixer and one for water; a thermometer, a watch and clean hands!

Your picture
You are going to make a photogram. Find lots of interesting objects around the house — scissors, old colour slides, drawing pins, spectacles, a bath chain, shapes of paper-things, in fact anything that will make an interesting silhouette picture. For *that's* what a photogam is!

What you do

1. Arrange your three trays on a table. The first should contain developer, which should be mixed with water at the correct temperature — look on the side of the bottle to see how much water and how warm the water should be. The second tray should contain water and the third, fixer — again, look on the side of the bottle for instructions.

2. Make sure your angle-poise lamp is pointed down at a right angle towards the table, then switch it off so that the only light is coming from the safe-light.

3. Take a piece of photographic paper out of its box and place it shiny-side up under the angle-poise. Then arrange your interesting objects on the piece of paper until you have a pleasing picture.

4. Switch on the angle-poise for about ten seconds. Then turn it off.

5. Take off your objects and immerse the paper in the first tray, making sure the paper is completely covered, for about 90 seconds. Then take out the paper, wash it quickly in the second tray, then immerse it in the third tray for about five minutes. You should now have a perfect photograph. You can now turn on the angle-poise and let your picture wash in a sink for a further 20 minutes before letting it dry in an airing cupboard.

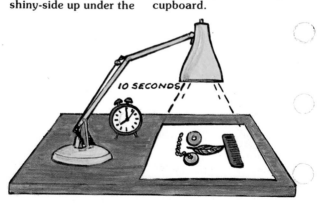

LIGHT

Did you know that photography actually means 'drawing with light'? The quality of light in your pictures is very important; it can make the difference between an ordinary picture and a very special one. However, there are many different forms of light, and each one will suit a particular type of photograph.

Time of day
The same scene will look incredibly different, depending on the time of day you take your picture. You can have fun by taking the same picture at different times of the day and then comparing the results!

Dawn Early in the morning there is very little dust and smoke so your pictures should be clear with a certain 'blueness'.

Noon The shadows are short and dark. There will be a 'whiteness' to your pictures.

Dusk A golden, yellowish look to your pictures. Shadows are soft and long.

Light from different angles
The direction of light makes a tremendous difference to the look of portrait pictures. Sometimes, if you can't avoid shadows on a face, then use your flash and it will 'fill in' all the unwanted shadows.

Front lighting: Makes people look flat.

By Top Floor Studio

Side-lighting: Has a 3-D effect.

By Top Floor Studio

Back lighting: Gives a halo effect.

By Top Floor Studio

Seasons

The same picture taken at different times of the year can be a very interesting project. Choose a subject which changes, like a tree by a river. As each season passes, the subject will change as well as the conditions of light.

Winter:

Spring:

Summer:

Flash

Sometimes there isn't sufficient light for your photograph and so you need to use a flash. There are two different types of flash; either flash-bulbs which you can buy in a camera shop, or your camera will have a built-in electronic flash. More expensive 35mm. cameras have detachable flash units.

Hints

* If you don't want your portraits to be spoilt by 'red eye', then put some tissue paper over the flash bulb.
* Make sure you have fresh batteries if you have a built-in flash. When replacing batteries, always change all the batteries.
* Make sure you are at the right distance; too near will give 'red eye', too far will mean that the light from the flash won't be strong enough.

WRITING FROM PHOTOS

Storytime

Choose a photograph and make it the 'starting point' for your own story. Copy the story out onto best paper and mount the photograph next to the story. Choose a picture that will really inspire you!

"Harry the pig lived in a snow-covered field in a small village. He had no friends and the snow made him even more cold and miserable . . ."

"The magical flying ship had been caught in the ice for days on end. The wicked witch had cast her evil spell. What was to be done to save her? . . ."

Poetry corner

You can try out a similar idea but this time you could write poetry. Choose a photograph carefully and try to think of a really good title. If you can't think of what to write, try an 'acrostic' poem. Here is an example;

The little girl
Hears the sound
of the sea
Everywhere she
stands

Spray on her little face
Each drop tastes salty
As the waves come a little nearer.

A Day in the Life...

Choose one day (it helps if the weather is good)
and take photographs throughout the day to show
a 'typical' day in your life or the life of a friend. Try
to have pictures from early in the morning to late
at night. It helps to have a flash, but it isn't
essential.

9 o'clock
*Richard goes out to
play in the snow.*

10.30
*Grandpa comes out
to help him clear the
path.*

And so on...

Crazy captions

Find some crazy pictures. Think of a really good
caption that will bring out the humour of the
photograph. Now you need to make your caption.
Get some thin white paper and cut out an oval
shape. The oval needs to be large enough for the
writing to fit and small enough to fit on the
photograph. Make your caption short and simple.

Glue it onto the
photograph. If you
then photocopy
the photograph, it
will look very
realistic.

*Quick! Get down
and hide!*

PETS

Pets and all other animals are great fun to photograph but you need to be patient if you want a really good picture. Here are some handy hints.

Be patient!

You may need to wait a long time before the time is right to photograph your pet hamster or a snake at the zoo. Don't get distracted by something else or you may miss your only chance. Keep your eyes pinned on your subject.

Food!

Have some food handy in your spare hand. This is not for feeding your pet, but to make it look up. There is nothing more boring than a photograph of a dog when you can't see its face and it's looking down at the ground with its eyes closed. Shake some food about and your pet will look alert!

At the Zoo

This is, of course, a great place for you and your camera but beware, a photograph of a tiger is not a good photograph unless it is a *good* photograph of a tiger. Too many zoo snaps are taken in shadows. Wait for the animal to come out into the light and make sure you are ready.

Get in close

Try to fill the frame of your camera with the animal. A picture of a baby rabbit seen from 20 metres will not make your friends say "aah". They will say "what am I supposed to be looking at?"

Try to photograph pets from unusual angles.

Here the cat is caught hiding behind the sofa catching the warm rays of a sunny afternoon. Always look for surprise in your pet portraits.

This cat is perfectly framed in the doorway of a pretty cottage. She has been startled by an 'intruder' (the photographer) and this has given her a lovely facial expression. As the photographer, you will need to be ready to snap the picture the moment the opportunity arises. ▶

▲

Animal pictures can be funny. Here the man at the farm zoo is imitating the facial expression of the goat. Both the animal and the human look rather silly. Notice that a chocolate bar is being used to tempt the goat away from its usual shy position.

This photograph is made more interesting by the sign saying 'do not tap on the window'. ▼

ON HOLIDAY

Not surprisingly the holiday months are the busiest months for processing laboratories. There are more photographs taken by people on their summer holidays than at any other time in the year, even Christmas!

A new camera

Many people want to buy a new camera to take away on holiday. There is nothing better than reliving the memory of a happy summer holiday on a cold winter evening, so to pack a camera in your travel bag is a must. But beware! Make sure you have tried and tested your new camera BEFORE you leave for your holiday:

*Do you know how to load and unload your film?

*Do you know where the battery compartment is?

*Do you know how to work the self-timer mechanism?

It is a very good idea to buy a 12 exposure film when you first buy your camera, then you can quickly see your results before you leave for your holiday.

At the seaside

Not surprisingly, the biggest cause of camera breakdown is sand!

Everybody wants to take their camera on the beach, but it is a very dangerous place to take your camera.

Sand: It can ruin the inner mechanism of your camera.

Sea: The combination of salt and water can be disastrous.

Sun: Excessive heat can spoil the film.

However, if you are careful, you can have great fun at the seaside with your camera.

If you are taking a portrait of someone playing on the beach, make sure you choose the right moment. Don't take the picture from too far away, or your subject becomes lost in the holiday crowd.

Beach huts are always good subjects for seaside photography. The colours are bright and the shapes are interesting. Try to find unusual angles. Never be satisfied with an ordinary picture. You may as well buy a postcard!

PANORAMA

Sometimes when you want to take a photograph of a really interesting scene like a mountain range or a row of lovely old houses, you will find that when you look through the viewfinder you can't fit the whole scene in! This is when you will need to take a *panoramic photograph*. This is a series of pictures that can be joined together to make one large picture. It's easy to do and great fun.

Here are some helpful hints

*Move your eyes steadily across your panorama before you take any pictures. This will help to remind you to keep your camera level when you take your pictures.

*Take your photographs from left to right, the same direction as reading a book. This will help you keep a steady hand. After your first picture, you will need to have about a third of your previous picture in each succeeding one. This 'overlap' will ensure you don't miss out any part of your panorama.

How to make your panorama

> **You'll need**
> Your photographs
> Masking tape
> Scissors
> Glue
> Card

1. Arrange your pictures. The second photograph should overlap the first, and so on. Try to match up the photographs as accurately as you can.
2. Place a small piece of masking tape over the photographs as you match them. When you have finished, turn the panorama over carefully onto the other side.

3. Place larger pieces of masking tape over the joins at the back. Your panorama is now secure and you can remove the small pieces of tape that are still covering the photographs.

CUT OFF TO LEVEL

4. Carefully cut the top and bottom of your panorama.

5. Mount your montage on dark card. If you want, you can frame it.

Funny panoramas

Take a panorama of a field or gently-rolling hill. Get a friend to stand in each frame. Don't be too far away or you might need to shout so that she can hear where you want her to stand next. When you have made the panorama, it will look like trick photography!

Montage

This is a similar idea to panorama. Instead of just taking a series of horizontal pictures, you also take them vertically so your picture can be massive.

A montage picture of a large country house.

DO's and DONT's

DO
Always carry your camera wherever you go, even if you feel it's a real nuisance. You never know when something might happen that is totally surprising and that's the time you wish you had got your camera. Suddenly a rainbow will appear in the sky or you will see a dog and a cat fast asleep together on a lawn with their paws wrapped round each other. Don't forget the camera!

DONT
Never hold your finger in front of the lens! This might sound a trifle obvious, but many famous photographers have slipped their finger in front of the lens at the critical moment and hey presto, instead of a photograph of the perfect sunset, you have the photo of the perfect dirty fingernail!

DONT
Never leave your camera lying on the beach, unless it is inside a case or carefully wrapped in a waterproof bag. Sand will scratch your lens and if it gets inside the mechanism, the whole camera might seize up. Even though some cameras are waterproof, it is not worth taking the risk of getting your camera wet. Salt water is especially damaging because the salt will rust any metal on your camera.

DO
Always try to carry a spare roll of film when you go out with your camera, maybe even two! Some camera bags are even fitted with extra space to fit a spare roll of film. Just imagine, you are about to take a totally brilliant photograph of a giraffe at the zoo . . . you press the shutter and nothing happens! By the time you have run to the gift shop (if there is one) and got an extra film, the giraffe has gone behind a brick wall taking a nap!

DO

Always carry a packet of lens' wipes with you. They are very soft tissues that clean your lens without damaging it. You can buy them from any good photographic shop and if you fold the packet you can tuck it inside your camera case. If ever you are stuck without them, then the next best thing to use is a very clean handkerchief, but make sure you rub gently. Never use your clothes or, even worse, toilet paper!

DON'T

Never take a flash photograph with your camera pointing towards a bright light. If you do, all the people in your picture will have very red eyes! To avoid 'red eye', make sure the bright light (it might be a fluorescent lamp in a kitchen at a party) is behind you when you take your photograph. This means that the people in your photograph will be looking at the light when you snap, so their pupils will be smaller and this will reduce 'red eye'.

DON'T

Never try to open the back of a camera when you can't remember if there is a film inside. Most modern cameras will tell you, but if you are still not sure, take the camera to a photographic shop and ask someone to check. They will probably put your camera into a special black bag that is light-proof and have a quick feel for you!

DO

Always keep very still when you take your photograph. This will stop your picture looking blurred. If it is windy outside and you want to take a picture, then try to lean your camera against a wall or something else solid. Another good idea is to breathe in just as you are going to 'click', then hold your breath when you are pressing the shutter.

CREATIVE IDEAS

Picture your favourite programme

Have you ever thought of photographing your favourite T.V. programme? You could build up a whole collection of such pictures. The bright light from a television means that you do not need to use a flash, either. In fact, a flash would bounce back off the glass of a T.V. screen and ruin your picture. You should use slow speed film, preferably 100ASA .

Photograph
* your favourite soap stars
* an exciting football match
* an old black and white film
* your favourite pop group

Greetings Cards

Why not make your own cards this year using your own photographs? All you need to do is to choose some suitable photographs for friends or relatives you have in mind. It will make a refreshing change from shop cards and can be a lot cheaper!

You'll need
Glue
Scissors
Coloured card
Ruler
Pens and pencils

What you do
1. Choose a photograph.
2. Cut out some card. It needs to be just larger than the photograph when it is folded in two.
3. Score the card with the edge of the scissors and the ruler.
4. Stick on your photograph so that the widest margin is at the bottom of the card.
5. Write your greetings message in bright letters on the front and inside the card.

FOLD

WISH YOU WERE HERE

Some ideas:
A photograph of a pet; a holiday scene; a new baby in the family; the garden on a lovely summer day, etc.

Upside Down

Here's a really unusual idea that can have great results and may really puzzle your friends. Ask a friend to hang upside down! This might sound crazy but if your friend does agree and you take a photograph, then you can stick it in your album the wrong way up and your friend will look really odd! It's especially good with long-haired friends because then it looks like their hair is standing on end as if they have just seen a ghost!

Good (and safe) places to hang upside down are a tree or climbing frame. MAKE SURE YOUR FRIEND DOES NOT HANG UPSIDE DOWN FOR TOO LONG!

A sea of faces

Here's a really good idea that will help you take a photograph of lots of friends at the same time. Ask four or five people to lie down on the ground (somewhere warm and dry) and to put all their faces together as if they were the hands of a clock. Stand up (it may be a good idea to stand on a small stool or a box) and take their photograph but only of their faces. Watch out for shadows and make sure they are all smiling and with their eyes open!

Picture teasers

Here's a game you can play with photographs, even parts of photos! Take some pictures of well-known objects from a distance and then take another picture of the same object but this time from close-up so that it only shows a small part of the object. Use a whole film (24exp.) so you will end up with 12 pairs of pictures. Jumble them up and see if your friends can guess which 'bit' belongs to which 'whole' object!

BLACK AND WHITE

Very few children take photographs with black and white film. Very few camera shops actually process and develop black and white film, so it's hardly surprising! These pages show you some of the advantages of black and white film over colour and explain how black and white film is developed and printed so that one day you will be able to do it yourself!

Black and white pictures create an atmosphere and a certain mood of their very own. The photographer is guided by the subject and not by choice of colour, so the subject of the picture stands out more clearly.

Graveyards are very atmospheric and moody places and black and white film really brings this out. The texture of the gravestones stand out really clearly.

Faces of old people stand out very clearly with black and white film. In this picture, the faces of the men seem to blend into the old wall of the building.

Developing black and white film

1. The film is taken off the cassette in a dark-room and put onto a spool.

2. The spool is placed into a light-tight black box.

3. Film developer is poured into the box and the box is sealed. The developer has to be at the right temperature and has to be mixed at the correct ratio with water.

4. The box is agitated (shaken vigorously) every 30 seconds until the film has developed. This usually takes about 6 minutes, depending on the type of film and the type of developer.

5. The developer is poured away and a film 'fixative' is poured into the box, which stops the film developing any further.

6. After the film is 'fixed', it has to be washed with running cold water for about 20 minutes to wash all the chemicals away.

7. The film is taken out of the box and off the spool. It hangs to dry in a special place, a little like an airing cupboard.

Printing black and white negatives

1. Your negatives are now ready to make prints from. They are cut into smaller, more manageable strips and a negative is chosen and put in an enlarger.

2. Once the negative is focused the light is switched off. A piece of photographic paper is placed underneath the negative and the light is switched on, allowing light to pass through the negative and onto the paper below, carrying with it the image of the negative, for about ten seconds.

3. The paper is placed in a tray of print developer for about 2 minutes. During that time, the print appears as if by magic on the paper.

4. The paper is dipped quickly in water and then into print 'fixative', which stops any more developing taking place.

5. The print is left to wash in running water for about 20 minutes, allowing all remaining chemicals to be washed away.

6. The print can now be dried in a drying machine, which again is rather similar to an airing cupboard. Before it is put in a dryer, any excess water is washed away using a small sponge or soft scraper.

Industrial buildings look very good in black and white.

FUN WITH SLIDES

Slides are brighter and truer to real life than any print but few photographers choose to use them, probably because you can't immediately see a slide, whereas you can immediately see a print. However, slides are really a lot more exciting than normal print and they can make any picture look really special!

Slide film

Most slide film is expensive but this normally includes the price of processing, so really, prices are comparable with prints. Your slide can be developed into a print at any time, just like a print negative, so do please care for your slides!

Helpful hints

* Always hold your slides at the sides, never in the middle. Not only will fingerprints spoil your slide show, they will also spoil any prints you make!
* Store your slides carefully. They will be returned from the processing laboratories in a dust-proof box.
* Use sticky labels to record the content of each box. This saves you having to take out the slides all the time.

Showing slides

1. Viewer

This is the cheapest method — some small viewers cost less than a week's pocket money. Battery-operated ones are better because you don't have to hold them up to the light. The light goes on automatically when you press the slide into the viewer. Always put the slide in with the little red dot in the top right hand corner, otherwise your picture will be the wrong way up.

2. Projector

You need a projector if you want to have a slide show, but quality and price can vary enormously. With the cheaper ones, you need to put the slides in manually, one at a time. The more expensive projectors have magazines which you can pre-load with the slides of your choice. You can also store slides in magazines instead of slide boxes.

Screens

White screens are very expensive. It helps to have a friend who will lend you one. If not, a white wall will do. Make sure the projector is on a sturdy table. If you don't have a white wall, then find a big poster and use the reverse side. Use those sticky pads, not Sellotape. You will never be forgiven if you leave marks on the wall!

Light box

A light box is a device to enable you to see slides at a glance so that you can prepare a slide show. They are expensive, but you can make your own if you are lucky enough to have a glass table. Cover the table with tracing paper and put white card underneath. Shine an angle-poise down on the table and you will be able to see your slides really clearly.

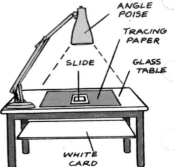

ANGLE POISE

TRACING PAPER

SLIDE

GLASS TABLE

WHITE CARD

UNUSUAL SHOTS

The single most important thing in becoming a really good photographer is to try to take the picture that no-one else thought of taking. You must always try to be original and to look at the world around you in a fresh and original way. This skill only comes with practice, so to help you get started, here are a few 'unusual' photographs that might give you some unusual ideas of your own!

Find something unusual to photograph in a crowded playground or park. Don't just photograph faces from a distance like everyone else. This picture of girls' legs on a bench captures the atmosphere of a school playtime in an unexpected way.

Try to look for contrasts of subject matter. There are plenty of examples in the world around you. Here it is the sharp contrast of a horse and the ugly industrial landscape behind.

One of the best times to take pictures is just after it has stopped raining. The light is often good and the fresh puddles on the ground give the photographer tremendous opportunities for reflections. This picture of an upside down St. Paul's Cathedral in a little side street is an unusual change from the usual picture postcards!

Reflections in glass can be very effective. Here, the viaduct that the train is passing over is reflected into the moving train, making a dramatic and surprising picture.

ACTION SHOTS

Sport

The top professional photographers take a wide variety of cameras and lenses to major sporting events like football and tennis matches. They also have access to the best positions, very near the centre of action. You will have seen photographers cramming the goalmouth at a football match.

So how can you be sure of taking good action shots at a sporting event when you only have one camera and have to sit with everyone else? Try these helpful hints . . .

1. Get in the best possible position before the start. If you aren't very tall then take a chair but make sure you don't block the view for someone else.

2. Try to take your action shots at the peak of activity eg. when a goal is being scored (or just after it has been scored) or when a high jumper is just clearing the bar.

3. Use a fast film (1000 ASA) so that your photograph won't be blurred. If there is fast action, then you need to use a method called panning to make sure your photograph isn't blurred. Follow the line of action with your camera, so that you are moving with the action. Remember to keep your camera steady, especially as you press the shutter.

The right position. You are as close as possible and you have waited for the peak of action. Timing is essential in action photography.

▲
Kites are good subjects of action shots because their colours stand out so well against the sky. Wait until the kite ribbon is stretched behind the kite — even better if it is in a spiral shape.

Get in close. A picture of a rock star from a distance is not an interesting picture, because he could be anybody!
▼

Peak of activity. You must wait for the best moment. This wave against the breakwater was at its highest point when

the picture was ▲ *taken. You must also think about getting in the right position so the picture is as dramatic as possible.*

Still life photography is the closest to drawing and painting. As the photographer, you are looking for shape, texture, form and colour.

Flowers

If you want to take a close up picture of a flower, it is a good idea to get a tray and use it as a windshield to stop the eventual photograph being blurred. Even on a very calm day, the slightest breeze will make the flower sway too much.

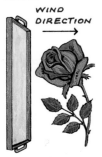

WIND DIRECTION →

Food

If you want to take a still-life photograph of food (maybe you are doing a food project at school) then arrange it carefully in front of a large piece of white card. This will help the different colours and textures of the food stand out a lot more clearly. If you are photographing fruit, brush on a thin coat of vegetable oil with a paint brush and this will make the fruit look really tasty (even though it would taste horrible!).

Look down on your subject. This piece of wood found on a beach looks much more effective as a still life picture because the photographer is looking directly down on the subject and this makes the picture more abstract.

Everyday objects like a pile of worn driftwood come across very well in a still life photograph, but only if you get in as close as possible and fill up the picture with the subject.

▼

Unusual angles. This is a picture of steps leading down to the sea but the layers of different textures give the picture an abstract quality. ▶

Ordinary everyday objects such as a garden table change their appearance to the eye after a heavy fall of snow. The table is now a strange, haunting object and photography captures this well.

▲

Negatives

Always handle your negatives very carefully. Store them somewhere dry and free from dust. The best place is a special drawer or a wooden box. Keep your negatives in the cover supplied by the processing laboratory. Buy some little plain stickers and number each pack of negatives, then in a separate book keep a written record of the date of each film and roughly what is on it!
eg. **7 March 1991**
Day at the seaside with *G*ran.

Your best photographs

When you get your photographs back from the processing laboratory, you will want to display them so you can show your friends. There are plenty of different ways of doing this but remember, be a little selective about which photographs you display. Not every photograph deserves to go in an album! Here are a few ideas:

1. Flip-up album

The prints slot into acetate envelopes. This is by far the cheapest way to display your pictures. Many postal photographic services send you these albums free of charge.

2. Album with pages covered with sticky acetate

These more expensive albums protect your photographs from sticky fingers and spilt drink but it can be a bit tricky to remove the prints.

3. Album with plain pages

This is the most expensive way to display your prints but it is the most professional and the most pleasing to the eye. Photographs need to be attached with glue (only a little) or photo corners which can be a bit fiddly!

Cropping

This is like giving a photograph a well-deserved haircut! Cropping is when you cut away any unwanted background so that you show only the really important parts of the photograph, as shown in this illustration. Score a line with a ruler and pencil and then cut as carefully as you can with some sharp scissors. However, the best thing to do is to bring to school the photographs you want to crop and ask your teacher nicely if you can use the paper cutter. This will give a much sharper edge but make sure you don't cut your picture in half!

Framing

You may want to frame your favourite photographs. You can buy clip frames quite cheaply. All clip frames come with a piece of quality paper that can be used as a 'mount' for your photograph. One side is white and the reverse side is black. Choose the colour which really makes your photograph stand out. If neither colour really works, then cut a piece of coloured paper of your own choice.

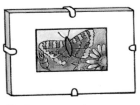

Enlargements

Most photographic laboratories can enlarge prints to a variety of standard sizes, even up to poster size. It is a good idea to choose 50% larger prints in the first place because then if you crop your picture, it is still a good size. One easy way of enlarging a picture is to take the original print to a shop that has a colour photocopier. It is quite expensive but cheaper than a laboratory, and more fun because you can see it happening!

LOOK AFTER YOUR CAMERA

If you look after your camera properly, you should get years and years of faithful service! You will get better, clearer pictures if you care for your camera. Here are a few helpful suggestions.

Lens
Use lens wipes to clean your lens. Never touch the lens with your hands. The oil on your fingers will cause serious damage. Never wash your lens. If you have a 35mm. camera, it is a good idea to buy a U.V. (ultra-violet) filter to cover and protect the lens.

Body
Use a soft cloth to wipe away dust and grease stains. Make sure it is dry. Do not let dust gather around the shutter or any other switches.

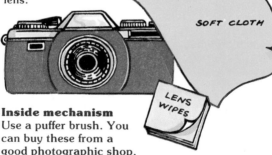

SOFT CLOTH

LENS WIPES

Inside mechanism
Use a puffer brush. You can buy these from a good photographic shop. You squeeze air through a soft brush. You should never blow directly at a camera as your breath is not always clean!

PUFFER BRUSH

Batteries

When your batteries need changing, change them both. Never mix types of batteries. Change batteries before they start to run down, or the electronic mechanisms on your camera will not function properly. If you leave your camera for a long period of time, take the batteries out. If they are left to corrode, they will cause serious damage to your camera.

Servicing your cameras

Most camera shops offer a comprehensive 'service' for your camera. Rather like a car service, every single aspect of your camera is checked. However, this servicing is only really recommended for the more expensive 35mm. and single-reflex cameras as the minimum charge for a service is quite expensive.

Insurance

If you have a reasonably good camera, make sure it is insured, either separately or on the general house insurance.

Never leave your camera in an obvious place. When not in use, keep it in its case and then make sure it's hidden from view. Take out an old film the moment it is used, then at least if your camera is ever stolen, the film will be safe!

At the Airport

Be careful at the check-in. The security system at all airports, where your luggage is checked, uses x-ray and this can seriously damage your film. So carry your camera separately.

Storage

Do not leave your camera in a hot place for too long, especially a hot car. Even a glove compartment is a bad place to store your camera because that, too, can overheat. The best place is probably under a seat.

Scrapbook

Have you ever been on holiday and collected things for a scrapbook? Tickets from railway journeys, menus from restaurants, postcards of castles . . . Why not add interest and originality to your holiday scrapbook by sticking in photographs amongst all your other memories?

Some ideas for your scrapbook:

* The view from the train to go with the railway ticket.

* Your family sitting at the table to go with the restaurant menu.

* Your own picture of the castle to go alongside the postcard!

The sun in your hand

Here's how to take a photograph that will mystify and confuse your friends. You need a lovely, clear summer evening and a setting sun that isn't too bright. Get a friend to stand in front of the sunset and ask him or her to hold out a hand in front of the sun. Look through the viewfinder of your camera. You need to arrange the hand until it looks like it's holding the sun. Get your friend to hold a tennis racket and the sun will look like a tennis ball!

How much have you changed?

It's amazing how quickly we are all changing and there's no better way of showing changes in people than by taking photos! If you have a little brother or sister, then try and photograph them at regular intervals — build up a whole collection of pictures and put them in a scrapbook.

Family Tree

Collect photographs of your family. Try to build up a family tree of portraits. Ask your grandparents, uncles and aunts. You can take the pictures of your own immediate family yourself. Get a large piece of paper or card and arrange the pictures. Try to get the best picture for each member of your family. Find out the dates of birth, death and marriage.

Crazy Captions

You might enjoy reading 'true life' photo comics but have you ever considered making your own? When you next have a party, take a whole roll of film that includes lots of photographs of people talking. Then take a good look at each picture and think up some amusing captions to go with each photograph. It can be great fun!

> **What you need:**
> Photos
> Scissors
> Glue
> Paper

Try and make the caption amusing. Put them all together to make your own little cartoon strip. Good luck!

Make your own family tree.

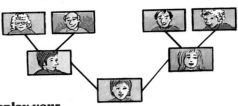

Display your photographs like this.

Camera bag

This is used for carrying your camera and equipment around. There are padded compartments for you to store lenses, filters and spare film. Camera bags have thick straps that make them reasonably comfortable to carry.

Cable release

Often when you are taking a photograph and you squeeze the shutter, you can accidentally jog the camera and spoil the picture. A cable release allows you to fire the shutter without actually touching the camera. It is a long and flexible cable that connects to the camera and when you press the end, it automatically operates the shutter mechanism on the camera; it's a little like pressing the button on a remote control in order to change a television channel.

Tripods

A tripod is particularly good for long exposures — that is when the shutter is open for an extended period of time — because camera shake can easily spoil your pictures. Most tripods have adjustable legs and an adjustable head to support the camera in different positions.

If you do not wish to carry a full-sized tripod around with you (which can be very cumbersome) then a useful alternative is a mini-tripod, which can stand on any rigid surface, even a small table.

Sepia toner

Have you ever seen very old family photographs that have an *'olde worlde'* brownish tinge? These are sepia photographs and it is very easy to sepia some of your own black and white photographs, as long as you buy some sepia toner which comes in little bottles from most photographic shops. You don't have to work in a darkroom, a kitchen will do, as long as you have trays for the toner, the fix and for the water!

> **Remember** — only black and white photographs and ask first if you are going to sepia old black and white photographs that belong to the family!

Lens cap

Whereas most automatic cameras have a sliding door to protect the lens, a 35mm, or single-reflex camera has its lens protected by a lens cap, which is removed before the photograph is taken, hopefully! Always leave the lens cap on when the camera is not in use.

Lens caps are very easy to lose so it is a good idea to buy a lens cap saver, which attaches the lens cap to the main body of the lens by way of a cord.

Tape recorder

If you are going to have a slide show, then why not record the commentary onto tape before you have the show?

You could record some lovely soft music, too, to go with slides of a sunset over the sea.

It doesn't have to be slides. Why not have a photographic exhibition in your bedroom of pictures of animals and play 'Carnival of the Animals' by Saint-Saens to go along with it? It would create a really special atmosphere. But I'm sure you will be able to think of your own exhibition!